You Are Not Alone
Families Touched By Cancer

by Eva Grayzel

*Dedicated to children who have
a family member with cancer*

Talk4Hope.com

You Are Not Alone, Families Touched by Cancer
Published by Eva Grayzel © 2010
4245 Farmersville Court
Easton, PA 18045
Contact & special orders: eva@evagrayzel.com

Printed in Pennsylvania

Grayzel, Eva
You Are Not Alone, Families Touched by Cancer / Eva Grayzel

Summary: Cancer changes family dynamics. Everyone in the family is affected. Misty and Monroe are learning how change in their Mom's health alters their daily routine. They need ideas and suggestions on how to adapt. Children from different countries around the world who have a family member with cancer share what they do to soothe sadness, ease tension and make things better.

ISBN# 978-0-9823857-0-8

Cancer, Juvenile literature
1. Cancer
2. Family
3. Communication
4. Children's Writing

Publisher Eva Grayzel www.evagrayzel.com
Design & Layout, Logo & Cover by Pierre Bohemond, Easton PA
Selected Photographs iStockphoto.com
Illustrations by Paul Fallaha, Clifton NJ

Somewhere, someone

feels as you do.

Meet the Martin family. Mrs. Martin has cancer. Mr. Martin tries very hard to be the best Dad he can be while his wife is managing her care. Their daughter Misty is six years old. Their son Monroe is four.

Monroe has a cold; a runny nose, sore throat, and cough. He is fighting an illness. If he rests, his cold will go away in a few days. But, these days he feels pretty rotten. His cold is contagious so he washes his hands a lot to prevent spreading his germs.

Mrs. Martin's illness is different. Hers is NOT contagious. Cancer doesn't pass through contact like a virus. Mrs. Martin's cancer may not go away for a few months, or years. But, she doesn't feel rotten ALL the time like Monroe does when he has a cold.

Sometimes, there are days that go by when Mrs. Martin feels fine even though she is having treatment for cancer. Sometimes, there are only moments when Mrs. Martin feels fine.

If you look inside her heart, you will see that Mrs. Martin loves her children more than anything and wants them to feel safe and secure.

Monroe and Misty are smart, just like you. They know when their Mom is pretending to be strong, even when she is aching inside and out.

Misty and Monroe have a hard time understanding
how their Mom's feelings affect her actions.
Has this scene happened in your home?

"Monroe, stop teasing your sister, I can't take it!"
Mrs. Martin calls out.
"She started," Monroe yells.

"No, he took this from me, and he didn't ask...
He makes me mad!" Misty shouts.

"That's it...go to your rooms!" hollers Mom,
" I don't want to see you until you can be nice."

Her actions don't show how she really feels in her heart.

Because she has cancer, Mrs. Martin has less patience and energy to solve the problem in a way that would make everyone feel better.

Can you think of a way to make things better?

Meet children from around the world
and how they cope with a family member who has cancer.

I'm Matias from Brazil.
My name means 'Gift from God.'

My Dad does everything possible to get better. Our daily routine is different because we never know if it will be a good day for him or not. I have a hard time talking about how it makes me feel. But, I'm really good at giving hugs.

I open my arms and hold Dad for a good long time. He tells me that my hugs are medicine. I don't worry about finding the right words. **I hug**.

What do you do when you don't know what to say?

I'm Maks from Russia.
My name means 'Great.'

My mother doesn't go to work anymore. Now, she spends her days getting radiation and chemotherapy treatments for her cancer, so it goes away for good.

When my sister and I get angry at each other, my mother raises her voice, more than ever before. I'm the big brother. I've learned that it helps to apologize right away. **I say "I'm sorry."**

Practice saying 'I'm sorry' this way:
   "I'm sorry you are not feeling well."
   "I'm sorry you have to fight cancer."
   "I'm sorry that I can't be perfect when
   things are hard for you."

Is it easy or difficult for you to say "I'm Sorry"?

I'm Malin from Hawaii.
My name means 'Peaceful.'

My aunt is not her usual self since her diagnosis. These days, **I give a back rub** to her every time I visit. It makes her relax. She knows I love her, even if I don't say it.

What could you do to help a family member with cancer feel better?

I'm Marceline from Canada.
My name means 'Young Warrior.'

I've been told crying is a good way to let out feelings. I feel sad and sometimes cry when I see how cancer has changed my Grandpa. Then I wipe my tears, put on the same strong mask that my Grandpa wears, and **I say, "I love you."**

Do you say "I love you" often enough?

I'm Mel from Australia.
My name means 'Honey.'

My brother has days when he is very weak and tired. I feel sad that I am well and he isn't. I wish I could wave a magic wand and make him better. When he has a rough day, **I call Grandma**. It helps me to tell her how I feel. She gives me good advice.

Who would you call?

I'm Masako from Japan.
My name means 'Justice.'

I see a counselor because my Mom has cancer and I am scared. I like talking to someone who doesn't live in my house, or know my family well. I can tell her anything and not worry I would hurt someone's feelings. She tells me my feelings are normal. She helps me cope.

Who do you talk to?

I'm Mohana from India.
My name means 'Enchanting.'

My sister Punita and I live with our grandparents. My sister has cancer and our parents work in a city far away to make enough money to pay for her treatment. She gets more attention lately, and I understand that.

I spend more time with friends. I'm lucky to have friends who call me, come over to play, and invite me places.

My friends help me through the hard times.

Who are your special friends?

13

I'm Mutazz from Saudia Arabia.
My name means 'Strong.'

Ever since my Mom got cancer, I choose to stay close to home, in case she needs me. When she is resting, I draw colorful pictures for her. Or, I go to the tree we planted together and I water it. I feel better after **I draw pictures or visit our garden**.

Have you tried drawing, visiting a garden
or planting a tree to soothe sadness?

I'm Marni from Morocco.
My name means 'To Rejoice.'

I love music and dancing. When Dad has energy, we dance in the living room. When he doesn't feel up to dancing, we listen to music together. When he needs quiet time, **I listen to music** through earphones and find new songs we can enjoy together.

If you could do something special with your relative who has cancer, what would you do?

I'm Malva from Greece.
My name means 'Delicate.'

I have cancer. My friend gave me this soft, pretty diary. I hide it in my drawer. I like to write when things feel tense in the house: a phone call from the doctor, a visitor who my Mom tells everything to and cries, when my parents argue about what to do... **I write**. It's amazing how much better I feel after writing out my feelings.

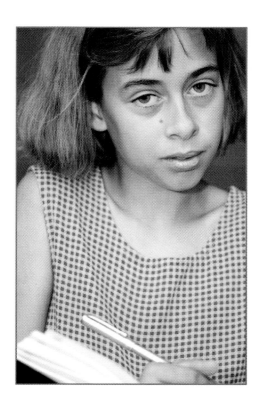

Do you have a special book to write in?

I'm Milek from Poland
My name means 'Lover of Glory.'

I pray every night that my brother gets better. I asked our religious leader what prayer I could say that would help him. He told me to pray for strength, courage, honesty, and lots of hugs and kisses for our whole family. Now, I feel my prayers make a difference.

Do you pray?

I'm Mahir from South Africa.
My name means 'Clever.'

My grades have been lower than usual. I'm always thinking about my Dad, even at school. Who would fix my bike? Who would be my basketball team's coach? Who would help me with math?

My parents told my teacher about Dad's cancer. She understands why I'm having a hard time focusing on school work.

I don't like getting low grades and giving my parents something else to worry about. **So, I get extra help with homework**.

Who helps you with homework?

I'm Merritt from Sweden.
My name means 'Small and Famous.'

My Mom was very grouchy for a long time. I thought she was mad at me. When I learned her tumor was cancer, I understood. She wasn't upset at me. She was just worried. To make things better, **I help out**.

I wash the dishes when they pile up. I fold the laundry. Mostly, I like helping my Mom get better. I remind her to take her medicine. I bring her water to drink, and fresh fruit for a healthy snack.

When I feel stress in the house, I say:
"What can I do to help?"

How could you help out?

There are many families everywhere in the world struggling with cancer.
You and your family have to work together and support each other through difficult times.

Always remember, you are not alone.

One day, the hardship of living with cancer will go away. Through difficult times, we grow as human beings. As we grow, we become wiser, more patient, and more understanding. You'll see.

These are wonderful qualities
and make us better people.

Your family needs YOU.

The person with cancer in your family
needs your hugs,
your smiles,
your thoughts in a card,
your pictures.

FROM MONROE
AGE 5

They need your wishes for a better year,

a better day,

a better moment.

MAIL

Children From Around The World

Can you remember the country they're from?

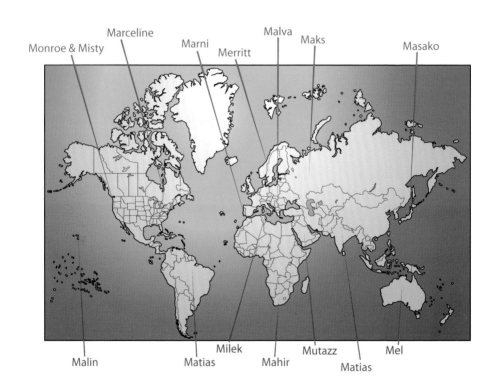

Marceline

Monroe & Misty

Marni

Merritt

Malva

Maks

Masako

Malin

Matias

Milek

Mahir

Mutazz

Matias

Mel

What does your name mean?
Why were you named that particular name?

Quick Reference Guide

Suggestions for children:
- Give hugs and back rubs often
- Say 'I love you'
- Apologize for upsetting someone you care about
- Talk to a counselor for advice
- Visit friends
- Draw and write to express your feelings
- Listen to music
- Pray for strength and courage
- Help out

Suggestions for parents:
- Keep markers and paper easily accessible for drawing
- Encourage writing in a diary
- Seek recommendations for a good therapist
- Inform school teachers about the illness
- Praise childen regularly and tell them you love them
- Ask your childen if they have any questions
- Talk about how you named your childen

Suggestions for families:
- Make a video and tell family stories
- Put together a photo album
- Enjoy community activities
- Do a kind act for someone in need
- Laugh often through jokes, games, stories
- Dance together
- Plant a tree or seeds for flower - watch them grow

Eva (left) and her family

About Author:
Eva Grayzel is a survivor of late stage oral cancer. She wrote the Talk4Hope children's book series to celebrate her 10-year anniversary cancer free. Despite having one third of her tongue reconstructed, Eva fortunately regained articulation of speech and continues her career as a performance artist while lecturing internationally telling her story about overcoming great odds. **Visit EvaGrayzel.com.**

Note from the Author:
My children were 5 and 7 years old when I was diagnosed with cancer. I wish I had sought professional counseling for my children who were deeply affected by watching me struggle with the serious effects of my treatment. Their fear of losing me was deep, real, and bottled. The "Talk4Hope" series suggests outlets for children to cope with their feelings.

Why the M's? When life takes a flip, we flip things around to meet the challenge. Turn Mom upside down and get Wow....that was my goal: Wow everyone with my smile. Focus on all the things I did have, not what I lost. What greater legacy to leave behind than a message through modeled behavior of courage and happiness in the face of adversity? During treatments, I continually surprised myself; even on my lowest days I could still find things in life that brought me joy.

About the Designer:
Pierre Bohemond is a multimedia artist (Music production, photography, and web/print design). His father Elie had lymphoma. Every visit, Pierre welcomed his father with a kiss, and always kissed his father goodbye. Elie's daily prayers, positive attitude and love of family kept him alive 16 years after his first chemotherapy treatment.

About the Illustrator:
Paul Fallaha is a freelance graphic artist & illustrator from Clifton, NJ. He is a representative of the New York Adobe® InDesign™ User Group. View his portfolio at www.fallahadesigns.com/paul/portfolio.

Special thanks to
Kenny, Jeremy and Elena
Elinor, Abby, Susan, Phyllis, Paul, Julie, Ellen
and Pierre

Eva Grayzel

- **Motivational Speaker**
  "Turning Adversity Into Opportunity"

- **Performance Artist**
  "Tales With A Twist"

- **Survivor Lecturer**
  "Tongue-Tied: Journey & Triumph over Oral Cancer"

Audience: Healthcare Professionals, Corporate, Educational, Community

Programs: Entertainment, Fundraiser, In-Service Training, Family Event

Book Eva
for your next
event/conference

Contact Program Coordinator:
programs@evagrayzel.com

www.EvaGrayzel.com